W9-ASB-841

CONTENTS

LAKE CLASSICS

Great American
Short Stories II

Edith
WHARTON

Stories retold by Emily Hutchinson
Illustrated by James McConnell

LAKE EDUCATION
Belmont, California

LAKE CLASSICS

Great American Short Stories I

Washington Irving, Nathaniel Hawthorne, Mark Twain, Bret Harte, Edgar Allan Poe, Kate Chopin, Willa Cather, Sarah Orne Jewett, Sherwood Anderson, Charles W. Chesnutt

Great American Short Stories II

Herman Melville, Stephen Crane, Ambrose Bierce, Jack London, Edith Wharton, Charlotte Perkins Gilman, Frank R. Stockton, Hamlin Garland, O. Henry, Richard Harding Davis

Great British and Irish Short Stories

Arthur Conan Doyle, Saki (H. H. Munro), Rudyard Kipling, Katherine Mansfield, Thomas Hardy, E. M. Forster, Robert Louis Stevenson, H. G. Wells, John Galsworthy, James Joyce

Great Short Stories from Around the World

Guy de Maupassant, Anton Chekhov, Leo Tolstoy, Selma Lagerlöf, Alphonse Daudet, Mori Ogwai, Leopoldo Alas, Rabindranath Tagore, Fyodor Dostoevsky, Honoré de Balzac

Cover and Text Designer: Diann Abbott

Library of Congress Catalog Number: 94-075026
ISBN 1-56103-018-X
Printed in the United States of America
1 9 8 7 6 5 4 3 2 1

❧ Lake Classic Short Stories ❧

"The universe is made of stories, not atoms."

—Muriel Rukeyser

"The story's about you."

—Horace

Everyone loves a good story. It is hard to think of a friendlier introduction to classic literature. For one thing, short stories are *short*—quick to get into and easy to finish. Of all the literary forms, the short story is the least intimidating and the most approachable.

Great literature is an important part of our human heritage. In the belief that this heritage belongs to everyone, *Lake Classic Short Stories* are adapted for today's readers. Lengthy sentences and paragraphs are shortened. Archaic words are replaced. Modern punctuation and spellings are used. Many of the longer stories are abridged. In all the stories, painstaking care has been taken to preserve the author's unique voice.

Lake Classic Short Stories have something for everyone. The hundreds of stories in the collection cover a broad terrain of themes, story types, and styles. Literary merit was a deciding factor in story selection. But no story was included unless it was as enjoyable as it was instructive. And special priority was given to stories that shine light on the human condition.

Each book in the *Lake Classic Short Stories* is devoted to the work of a single author. Little-known stories of merit are included with famous old favorites. Taken as a whole, the collected authors and stories make up a rich and diverse sampler of the story-teller's art.

Lake Classic Short Stories guarantee a great reading experience. Readers who look for common interests, concerns, and experiences are sure to find them. Readers who bring their own gifts of perception and appreciation to the stories will be doubly rewarded.

❦ Edith Wharton ❧
(1862–1937)

About the Author

Edith Newbold Jones was born in New York City. Her family was rich enough to hire tutors for her. A friend of hers once said, "All the studying she did was while her hair was being brushed."

She knew French, German, and Italian, and often traveled in England and Europe. She was definitely an "insider" in New York society. In writing about that society, she criticized it as rigid and stale. "A little world so well-ordered and so well-to-do does not often produce either eagles or fanatics," she once said.

At age 23, she married Edward Wharton, a man 12 years older than she. He turned out to have mental problems. Although divorce was not common then, they were divorced after 28 years of marriage.

Edith Wharton moved to Paris in 1907, and there she lived a wonderful life. She wrote in the mornings and entertained friends in the afternoons. One of her closest friends was the American novelist, Henry James. She took regular "motor-tours" of Italy, France, Germany, Austria, Spain, and Morocco. During World War I, her relief work in Paris earned her the cross of the Legion of Honor. She was living in Paris when she died of a stroke. As her coffin was carried down the street, the French flag was dipped in her honor.

A skillful social critic, Edith Wharton was also at her best in the supernatural world. Her ghost stories rank among the best in American literature. Wharton's characters were rich and well-educated. Her stories showed that even these people have their problems. Read Edith Wharton for a glimpse into a world that might surprise you.

The Pomegranate Seed

Who could be sending the mysterious letters? Mrs. Ashby had always trusted her husband, but now she's getting worried. Is someone trying to ruin their happy marriage?

HE DID NOT OPEN THE LETTER RIGHT AWAY. THE COLOR
SLOWLY LEFT HIS FACE.

The Pomegranate Seed

I

Charlotte Ashby stood on her doorstep. She stopped for a moment before putting her key in the lock. Until recently, this had been her favorite time of day. Since her marriage to Kenneth Ashby, she had enjoyed returning to the quiet house in the early evening. It was always such a pleasure to leave the noise of New York behind. The home she and Kenneth shared seemed like an island of peace in the very heart of the hurricane. In the last few months, however, everything had changed. Now she had to force herself to enter her own house.

She thought of only one thing—the letter she might or might not find on the hall table. Until she knew whether or not it was there, her mind had no room for anything else. The letter was always the same. It came in a square gray envelope with "Kenneth Ashby, Esquire," written on it. The handwriting was bold, but the ink was very faint. It looked as if there were not enough ink in the pen. Or perhaps the writer was very weak. Charlotte knew that the writing was that of a woman. Something about the style made Charlotte sure that a woman had written it.

The envelope never had anything on it but Kenneth's name. There was no stamp or address. The letter had to have been delivered by hand. The question was—whose hand?

No doubt that *someone* had put it in the mailbox. No doubt that the maid had taken it out and put it on the table. And it was always in the evening, after dark, that Charlotte saw it lying there. Since her marriage a little over a year ago, there had been seven of these letters. All the letters were just alike in appearance. In her mind, they had all become one letter—"it."

The first one had come the day after they got back from their honeymoon. The couple had been gone for more than two months. As they entered the house, the gray envelope was there on the hall table. Her eye fell on it before Kenneth's. Her first thought was, "Why, I've seen that writing before," but she could not remember where.

Charlotte wouldn't have thought twice about it, except for one thing. She happened to be looking at her husband when he first saw the letter. It all happened in a flash. He picked up the letter and raised it to his near-sighted eyes to read the faint writing. Then he quickly put the letter into his pocket. He didn't say one word. Charlotte had expected him to open it, but he didn't. Shortly after that, he said, "I've got a splitting headache. Do you mind if I go to bed early?"

That was the first time. Since then, Charlotte had never been present when he had received the letter. It usually came before he got home from his office. She always went upstairs and left it lying on the table. But even if she didn't see the letter, she could tell that it had come. All she had to do was look at his face. After reading the letter, he looked years older, emptied of life and courage. He hardly even knew that Charlotte was there. Sometimes he was silent for the rest of the evening. If he did speak at all, it was to scold Charlotte in some small way.

At such times, Charlotte would remember what her friends had said. They had warned her when she became engaged to Kenneth. "Marrying a heartbroken widower! Isn't that a little risky? Don't you remember his first wife? You know how Elsie Ashby used to run his life!"

Charlotte had taken it as a joke. "He may be glad of a little freedom for a change," she had laughed.

Then Charlotte and Kenneth got back from their honeymoon. Her friends were surprised at their happiness. "What have you done to Kenneth?" they had said. "He looks 20 years younger."

"I suppose I've taken him out of his rut," she had said with a smile.

But then the gray letters began to arrive. Even though Charlotte was sure the handwriting was a woman's, she didn't suspect he was being unfaithful. She was too sure of her husband's love to think such a thing. It was much more likely, she thought, that the letters were from a client. Perhaps he did not want a secretary to open them. Yes, that was why the letters had been carried to the house, Charlotte thought. And the client must be causing Kenneth a lot of trouble—judging from the effect the letters had on him. But Charlotte thought it odd that he had never once mentioned a troublesome client.

Then Charlotte thought about another possibility. Maybe the letters were coming from an old love. But that did not

seem likely. Charlotte's friends had told
her that Kenneth had never looked at
another woman after he first saw Elsie
Corder. Everyone knew how attached
he had been to his wife. An old love was
just about impossible. In fact, her friends
told her that her biggest problem would
be measuring up to Elsie. They said,
"He'll never let you move a piece of
furniture. He'll compare whatever you
try to do with what Elsie would have
done in your place."

None of these fears had come true. Two
years after his first wife's death,
Kenneth had fallen in love with her,
Charlotte Gorse. Ever since then, he had
been nothing but tender and loving. He
had spoken to her about his first wife
before their engagement. He told her
about his despair after the sudden death.
They had been married 12 years. But
even then, he did not believe that his own
life was over. When he met Charlotte, he
said that the future held new promises
for happiness.

After their honeymoon, Kenneth apologized for not being able to afford to redo the house. He told Charlotte to move the furniture around any way she liked. And as time went by, Charlotte felt more at ease in the house. She was more comfortable than she would have thought possible.

Charlotte had been so happy with her new life! Now she could not understand her new feelings of uneasiness. Key in hand, she stood on the doorstep, thinking. "What am I worrying about? There hasn't been a letter for three months now. Why should I imagine there's going to be one tonight?"

There was no reason to be upset. Yet there were days when she would stand outside for a long while, cold and shivering. Somehow she was certain that she would find a letter. Most of the time, when she opened the door and went in, there was nothing. But still— ever since the last letter had come—she had felt uneasy every evening. She never opened the door without thinking the letter might be there.

"I can't stand it! I can't bear another day of this!" she cried to herself. Then she turned the key in the lock and went in. There, on the table, lay another letter.

II

Charlotte was almost glad to see it. It seemed to give a reason for her feelings of uneasiness. What a fool she had been to ever doubt that it was from an old love! She picked up the envelope and held it against the light. Inside she saw the outline of a folded sheet. She knew that now she would have no peace until she found out what was written on that paper.

Her husband had not come in. He wouldn't be home for at least another 30 minutes. She would have time to take the letter upstairs to her sitting room. There, she could hold it over the teakettle until the steam loosened the glue on the envelope. When she had solved the mystery, she could replace the letter where she had found it. No one would be the wiser, and her curiosity would be satisfied.

She had another choice, of course. That was to simply *ask* her husband about the letter. Yet somehow it seemed even more difficult to do that. She had started to go up the stairs with the envelope. But then she came back down again and put it on the table.

"No, I just can't do it," she said to herself, disappointed.

What should she do, then? She couldn't just go on as usual. How could she have some tea and read her mail as if the letter weren't there? Suddenly she decided. She would wait in the library and see for herself. She would see with her own eyes what happened when he saw the letter. When he thought he was alone, he might give some sign. She wondered why she hadn't thought of this before! By leaving the door slightly open and sitting in the corner behind it, she could watch him. She drew a chair into the corner, sat down, and waited.

Finally she heard Kenneth's key in the door. She jumped up. The impulse to rush out and greet him almost made her forget why she was there. But then she remembered in time and sat down again. From her chair, she saw him enter the hall and take the key from the door. Then he took off his hat and coat. When he turned to throw his gloves on the hall table, he saw the envelope.

The light was full on his face. What Charlotte first noticed there was a look of surprise. It was clear that he had not expected the letter. But now that he saw it—he knew well enough what was in it. He did not open it right away, but simply stood still. The color slowly left his face. It seemed that he could not make himself touch the letter.

But finally he put out his hand and opened the envelope. Then he carried it into the light. In doing so, he turned his

back on Charlotte. Now she could see
only his bent head and slightly stooping
shoulders. All the writing must have
been on one page, for he did not turn the
sheet over.

Kenneth continued to stare at the
letter. He looked at it long enough to
have read it a dozen times. At least, it
seemed that way to Charlotte. Then she
saw him move. He raised the letter still
closer to his eyes, as if to see it better.
Then he lowered his head, and she saw
his lips touch the sheet.

"Kenneth!" she cried out to him as she
stepped into the hall.

The letter in his hand, Kenneth turned
and looked at her. "Where were you?" he
said in a low voice. He talked like a man
awakened from his sleep.

"In the library, waiting for you." She
tried to keep her voice calm. "What's
the matter! What's in that letter? You
look terrible."

He quickly slipped the letter into his
pocket. "Terrible? I'm sorry. I've had a

hard day in the office. I *do* look dog-tired, I suppose."

"You didn't look tired when you came in. It was only when you opened that letter!"

Charlotte looked very closely at her husband. She didn't want to trick him into telling her anything he wanted to keep a secret. Her only wish was to find out what the mystery was. And she wanted to find some way to help him if she could. "Even if it *is* another woman," she thought.

"Kenneth," she said, her heart beating fast, "I waited here on purpose to see you come in. I wanted to watch you while you opened that letter."

A look of anger crossed his face. "Ah, so you're in the habit of hiding now? You like to watch people open their letters when they don't know you're there?"

"Not in the habit. I never did such a thing before. But I had to find out what she writes to you in those gray envelopes."

"Why do you assume it's a woman?"

"It's a woman's handwriting. Are you saying it's not?"

"No, I'm not saying that. Well, since you must know, she writes to me about business."

"Legal business?"

"In a way, yes. Business in general."

"You take care of her business affairs for her?"

"Yes, I've done so for a very long time."

"Kenneth, dearest, won't you tell me who she is?"

"No. I can't. Professional secrecy."

The blood rushed from Charlotte's heart to her face. "Don't say that—don't!"

"Why not?"

"Because I saw you kiss the letter."

For a moment, Kenneth seemed unable to speak. Then he stammered out, "The writing is very faint. You must have seen me holding the letter close to my eyes. I could hardly read it."

"No—I saw you kissing it." He was silent. "Didn't I see you kissing it?"

He sank back, not seeming to care anymore. "Perhaps," he said.

"Kenneth! You stand there and say that—to me?"

"What possible difference can it make to you? The letter is about business, as I told you. Do you think I'd lie about it? The writer is a very old friend whom I haven't seen for a long time."

"Men don't kiss business letters—even from women who are very old friends. Not unless they have been in love, and are sorry to be apart."

"Well, it's not like that, my dear."

"No? Then prove it to me, darling. It's so easy! Just show me the letter!"

He pulled away from her and shook his head.

"You won't?"

"I can't."

"Then the woman who wrote it is your mistress."

"No, dear. No."

"Not now, perhaps. I suppose she's trying to get you back. You're fighting it, out of pity for me. My poor Kenneth!"

"I swear to you that she never was my mistress."

Charlotte felt the tears rushing to her eyes. "Then what is going on, Kenneth? What about me? Haven't you been happy this past year? Haven't I made you forget Elsie?"

She very rarely said his first wife's name. Now she tossed it out as if she were tossing a dangerous bomb into the open space between them. Then she stood back, waiting for it to explode.

Her husband did not move. His face grew sadder. "I have never forgotten Elsie," he said. Moments later, he said, "I've got a blinding headache."

"Ah, yes, the gray-envelope headache!"

She saw the surprise in his eyes. "I'd forgotten how closely I've been watched," he said coldly. "If you'll excuse me, I think I'll go up and try an hour in the dark. Maybe I can get rid of this headache."

"I'm sorry your head aches," she answered. "But before you go, I want to say something. Sooner or later this question must be settled between us.

Someone is trying to separate us. I don't care what it costs me to find out who it is."

She looked him right in the eyes. "If it costs me your love, I don't care! If I can't have your confidence, I don't want anything from you."

He looked at her sadly. "Give me time."

"Time for what? All you have to do is tell me her name."

"Time to show you that you haven't lost my love or my confidence."

"Well, I'm waiting."

He turned toward the stairs, and then glanced back at her. "Oh, please do wait, my love," he said, and went upstairs.

She heard his bedroom door close. Then she dropped into a chair and buried her face in her folded arms. "Why did I say that I didn't care if it cost me his love? What a lie!" She started to follow him so she could take back the foolish words. But she stopped suddenly, as she realized what had happened. He had had his way, after all. He had kept his secret to himself. And now he was shut up alone in his room, reading that other woman's letter.

III

Charlotte sat for a while in the library. The maid came in to ask about dinner, and Charlotte said that she was not hungry. A little snack later on would be enough.

She thought about the conversation she had just had with Kenneth. It seemed as if it were a dream. In her past year with Kenneth, he had shown only deep devotion and great tenderness. How ridiculous that a few moments ago she had accused him of an affair with another woman! But, then, what did the letters mean?

Again she felt she should go up to him. She wanted to beg his forgiveness, and laugh about the misunderstanding. But she didn't want to intrude on his privacy. She knew that he was troubled and unhappy. But he had clearly shown her that he wanted to fight out this battle alone. So she went up to her own room.

How strange it felt to be there—in the next room to his—and yet so far away! Now she felt sorry that she had not opened the letter before he came in. At least she would have known what his secret was.

Suddenly she had the idea of going to his mother. Charlotte was very fond of old Mrs. Ashby. There had been good feelings between them from the day they met. But the idea of talking to her seemed almost like a betrayal of Kenneth. What right did she have to tell anyone else about Kenneth's secret?

She was still wondering what to do when there was a knock on her door. Kenneth came in, dressed for dinner. He seemed surprised to see her sitting there, with her evening dress lying on the bed.

"Aren't you coming down?" he asked.

"I thought you were ill and had gone to bed," she said.

He forced a smile. "I'm not feeling very well, but we'd better go down." His face looked calmer than it had an hour earlier. She rang the maid and said that dinner should be prepared after all.

Soon dinner was served, and they sat down to it. At first, neither seemed able to find a word to say. But Kenneth then began to talk. He rambled on about politics, an art exhibit, and the health of an old aunt. All the while Charlotte watched him. "How tired he is! How terribly overtired!" she thought.

After dinner, they had some coffee. "You must go to bed early," Charlotte said. "You look so tired. They must overwork you at the office."

"I suppose we all overwork at times."

She rose and stood before him. "Well, I'm not going to have you working so hard. It's foolish. I can see you're ill." She put her hand on his forehead. "My poor old Kenneth. Prepare to be taken away soon on a long holiday."

He looked up at her. "A holiday?"

"Of course. Didn't you know I was planning to carry you off? We're going to leave in two weeks on a month's voyage to somewhere or other. On any one of the big cruising steamers." She kissed him on the forehead. "I'm tired, too, Kenneth."

He looked up at her. "Again? My dear, we can't. I can't *possibly* go away."

"I don't know why you say 'again,' Kenneth. We haven't taken a real holiday this year."

"Well, I simply can't go anywhere. I'm much too busy. Don't ask me to, dear."

Charlotte looked at her husband, puzzled. "I don't understand," she said.

"Don't try to," he muttered.

"Not try to?"

"Not now—not yet." He put up his hands and pressed them against his temples. "Can't you see that I mean it? I *can't* go away—no matter how much I might want to."

Charlotte looked at him closely. "The question is, *do* you want to?"

He returned her look for a moment. Then his lips began to tremble. He said, in a low voice, "I want whatever you want."

"And yet—"

"Don't ask me. I can't leave. I can't!"

"You mean that you can't get out of reach of those letters!"

Her husband had been standing in front of her. Now he turned away. He walked up and down the length of the room. As he did so, he kept his head bent and his eyes fixed on the carpet.

"It *is* that, isn't it?" Charlotte said. "Why not admit it? You can't live without those letters."

He continued pacing, and then he stopped suddenly and dropped into a chair. He covered his face with his hands. From the shaking of his shoulders, Charlotte saw that he was weeping. She had never seen a man cry, except her father when her mother had died. She had been just a little girl then, but she remembered how much the sight had frightened her. She was frightened now. She felt that she had to do something to help him.

"Kenneth! Kenneth!" she cried out. "Won't you listen to me? Can't you see that I'm suffering? If those letters hadn't had such an effect on you, I may never have noticed them. What I can't bear is to see how you dread the letters—how they make you suffer. Yet at the same time you can't live without them. You won't go away for fear of missing one.

"Or maybe she has actually *forbidden* you to leave. Kenneth, you must answer me! Is that the reason? Is it because she's forbidden you to leave that you won't go away with me? Kenneth, is that it? She won't let us go away together?"

Still he did not speak or even look up. A feeling of defeat swept over her. "You don't have to answer. I see that I'm right," she said.

Suddenly, he grabbed her hands. He pressed them so tightly that her rings cut into her flesh. It was the clutch of a man who felt himself slipping over a cliff. He was staring at her now as if she alone could save him. "Of course we'll go away together. We'll go wherever you want," he said in a low, confused voice. Then he put his arms around her, drew her close, and pressed his lips on hers.

IV

Charlotte had said to herself, "I shall sleep tonight." Instead, she sat before her fire into the small hours. She listened for any sound from her husband's room. But he seemed to be resting quietly. Once or twice she peeked in through his open door. She saw him stretched out in heavy sleep. "He's ill," she thought. "And it's not from overwork. It's this mysterious letter-writer."

She felt relieved that he had agreed to go on a trip. If only they could leave at once! She knew it would be useless to ask him to go right away. Meanwhile, the secret letter-writer would continue to work against her. She would have to fight against this invisible enemy every day until they left on their trip.

But once she got Kenneth away—and all to herself—she knew she could help him. Somehow she would release him from the evil spell he was under. Thinking these happy thoughts, she was finally able to get to sleep.

When she woke up, it was much later than her usual hour. She sat up in bed, surprised and a bit angry at having overslept. She liked to share breakfast with her husband, but today she had missed it. Just to be sure, she went into his room, but his bed was empty.

She called the maid and asked if Mr. Ashby had already gone. Yes, nearly an hour ago, the maid said, but he had left a message. He said to tell Mrs. Ashby that he was going to see about their tickets. Would she please be ready to sail tomorrow?

Charlotte said, *"Tomorrow?* You're sure he said we'd be sailing tomorrow?"

"Oh, ever so sure, ma'am."

"Well, it doesn't matter. Draw my bath, please," Charlotte said. She was in a wonderful mood. Winning such a victory made her feel young again. He loved her, then, as much as ever! He had understood that their happiness depended on their getting away at once. The morning danced along. She ordered a particularly good dinner, had her trunks brought down, and got ready to pack. She told the maid to get out some summer clothes, for of course they would be heading for sunshine.

Then it came to her that she didn't really know where they were going. She looked at the clock and saw that it was close to noon. She decided to call Kenneth at work. But the secretary told her that Mr. Ashby wasn't there. He had come in for a moment and then gone out again. He had said that he was going out of town.

Out of town! Charlotte hung up the phone and sat staring into space. Why had he gone out of town? And where had he gone? And of all days—why would he leave on the day before their holiday? She felt a faint shiver of uneasiness. Of course he had gone to see that woman— no doubt, to get her permission to leave.

Suddenly Charlotte's good mood was completely ruined. Then, little by little, she began to feel better. After all, her husband was doing what *she* wanted, not what the other woman wanted. Perhaps he had some business matters to wind up. There was no reason to assume that he was visiting the writer of the letters. No doubt he was with a client. She decided to go on getting ready for the trip.

When she finally noticed the time, it was five o'clock. And she had no idea where they were going the next day! She called her husband's office. The secretary said that Mr. Ashby had not been there since early morning.

Then she decided to call her mother-in-law. Of course! On the eve of a month-long trip, Kenneth would have gone to see her. Happily, she called up Mrs. Ashby. Hearing her friendly voice, Charlotte said, "Well, did Kenneth's news surprise you? What do you think of our trip?"

But Mrs. Ashby had not seen her son. She had not heard from him, and knew nothing about the trip. So Charlotte explained their sudden decision to Mrs. Ashby. As she did so, she became confident again that nothing could ever come between Kenneth and herself. Mrs. Ashby was glad to hear the news. She, too, had thought that Kenneth was looking worried and overtired. She agreed that a trip was the best thing for him.

"I'm always so glad when he gets away. Elsie hated traveling. She was always finding some reason to keep him from going anywhere. With you, thank goodness, it's different." Mrs. Ashby wasn't surprised that her son hadn't told her about the plans. She said he must have been in a rush from the moment the decision was made. No doubt he'd stop by on his way home for dinner. Mrs. Ashby invited Charlotte over. "No doubt he'll turn up while you're here," she said. Charlotte said she'd be over in a little while.

At about seven the telephone rang, and Charlotte ran to it. Now she would know! But it was only the secretary. He was calling to say that Mr. Ashby hadn't been back, or sent any word. Maybe by this time, Charlotte thought, he would be at his mother's. She put on her hat and coat. On her way out, she told the maid that she was going over to her mother-in-law's.

Mrs. Ashby lived nearby. As Charlotte walked through the cold spring evening, she imagined that every advancing figure was her husband's. But she did not meet him on the way, and he was not at his mother's. Kenneth had neither telephoned nor dropped by.

Old Mrs. Ashby sat by her bright fire. Her knitting needles were flashing in her busy hands. She assured Charlotte as best she could. When she asked what time they were sailing the next day, Charlotte had to say that she didn't know. Even Mrs. Ashby thought this was odd, but she said that it only showed what a rush he was in.

"But, Mother, it's nearly eight o'clock! He must realize that I've got to know when we're leaving tomorrow."

"Oh, the boat probably doesn't sail till evening. Sometimes they have to wait until midnight for the tide. Kenneth's probably counting on that. After all, he has a level head."

Charlotte stood up. "It's not that. Something has happened to him."

"Now, now, my dear. Don't worry for no reason. Why don't you stay and have dinner with me? He's sure to drop in here on his way home."

Charlotte called up her own house. The maid said that Mr. Ashby hadn't come in and hadn't telephoned. She would tell him where Charlotte was as soon as he came in. Charlotte followed Mrs. Ashby into her dining room, but she had no appetite. She watched as her mother-in-law had her dinner. Then they returned to the sitting room for a little while. At last, Charlotte got up and said, "I'd better go back. At this hour, Kenneth will certainly go straight home."

Mrs. Ashby smiled. "It's not very late, my dear."

"It's after nine," said Charlotte. "The fact is, I can't keep still."

Mrs. Ashby put aside her knitting and stood up. "I'm going with you," she said. Charlotte said that it was too late for the older woman to be going out. But Mrs. Ashby had made up her mind. They took a taxi to Charlotte's house. As soon as they drove up, Mrs. Ashby said, "You'll see. There will be a message."

But alas, there was no message. As Charlotte turned to take off her hat and coat, her eyes fell on the hall table. There lay a gray envelope with her husband's name in that faint handwriting. "Oh!" she cried out.

"What is it, my dear?" Mrs. Ashby asked.

Charlotte did not answer. She picked up the envelope and stared at it. Then an idea came to her. She turned and held out the envelope to her mother-in-law.

"Do you know that writing?" she asked.

Mrs. Ashby took the letter, adjusted her glasses, and lifted the envelope to the light. "Why!—" she exclaimed, and then stopped. Charlotte noticed that the letter shook in her usually steady hand. "But this is addressed to Kenneth," Mrs. Ashby said, in a low voice. Her tone seemed to hint that the letter was none of her business.

"Yes, it is addressed to him. But I want to know—do you know the writing?"

Mrs. Ashby handed back the letter. "No," she said firmly.

The two women went into the library. Charlotte turned on the light and closed the door. The envelope was still in her hand.

"I'm going to open it," she announced.

She caught her mother-in-law's surprised look. "But, Charlotte—a letter not addressed to you? My dear, you *can't*!"

"As if I cared about that—now!" She continued to look at Mrs. Ashby. "This letter may tell me where Kenneth is."

Mrs. Ashby said, "Why should it? What makes you think so? It can't possibly—"

Charlotte stared at her mother-in-law. "Ah, then you *do* know the writing?" she demanded.

"Know the writing? How should I? With all the people my son writes to... What I *do* know is—" Mrs. Ashby broke off, almost timidly. She stared at Charlotte.

Charlotte caught her by the wrist. "Mother! What do you know? Tell me! You *must*!"

"The only thing I know is that no good ever came of spying. A woman should never open her husband's letters behind his back."

The words made Charlotte laugh. She dropped her mother-in-law's wrist. "Is that all?" she said. "No good can come of this letter, opened or unopened. I know that well enough. But whatever happens, I mean to find out what's in it." Her hands had been shaking, but now they grew steady. And so did her voice.

"This is the ninth letter that has come for Kenneth since we've been married. All have been addressed in the same hand. All have been in these same gray envelopes. After each one arrives, he acts like a man who has had a terrible shock. It takes him hours to get back to normal.

"I've told him that I must know who is writing them. I can see that the letters are killing him. But he won't answer my questions. He says he can't tell me anything about the letters. Then last night he promised to go away with me—to get away from them."

Mrs. Ashby, with shaking steps, had walked to an armchair and sat down. "Ah," she said.

"So now you understand—"

"Did he tell you it was to get away from them?"

"He said, to get away—*to get away*. He was sobbing so that he could hardly speak. But I told him I knew what he had to get away from."

"And what did he say?"

"He took me in his arms and said he'd go wherever I wanted."

"Ah, thank goodness!" said Mrs. Ashby. There was a long silence. At last she looked up and spoke. "Are you sure there have been nine letters?"

"Perfectly. This is the ninth. I've kept count."

"And he has refused to explain?"

"Absolutely."

Mrs. Ashby spoke through pale lips. "When did they begin to come? Do you remember?"

Charlotte laughed again. "Remember? The first one came the night we got back from our honeymoon."

"That long ago?" Mrs. Ashby lifted her head and spoke with sudden energy. "Yes, open it."

The words were such a surprise that Charlotte felt the blood pounding in her temples. Her hands began to shake again. She found her husband's letter opener and ran it under the flap of the envelope. In the deep silence of the room, the tearing of the paper sounded like a human cry. She drew out the sheet and carried it to the lamp.

"Well?" Mrs. Ashby asked in a whisper.

"I can't make it out," she said. "The writing is too faint. Wait." She got a magnifying glass and held it over the letter.

"Well?" Mrs. Ashby asked again.

"It's no clearer. I can't read it."

"You mean the paper is an absolute blank?"

"No, not quite. There *is* writing on it. I can make out something like 'mine' and 'come.' It might be 'come.' It's so hard to tell."

Mrs. Ashby stood up suddenly. Her face was even paler than before. "Let me see," she said.

"She *knows*," thought Charlotte, as she pushed the letter across the table. Her mother-in-law bent over the sheet, without touching it with her hands. The light of the lamp fell directly on her old face. And Charlotte looked at her closely. She had never seen such a look! Her mother-in-law's face showed fear and hatred, dismay and anger. Finally, she looked up. "I can't. I can't," she said in a childish voice. Charlotte saw two tears roll down her cheeks.

"You *do* know the writing," Charlotte insisted.

Mrs. Ashby looked around the room. "How can I tell? I was surprised at first . . ."

"Surprised by the writing?"

"Well, I thought—"

"You'd better say it out, Mother! You knew at once it was *her* writing?"

Her mother-in-law leaned against the table. Her voice was sad. "But we're going mad. We're both going mad. Both of us know that such things are impossible."

Charlotte looked at her with pity. "For a long time now I've known that anything is possible."

"Even this?"

"Yes, exactly this."

"But this letter—after all, there's nothing in this letter."

"Perhaps there is something in it to him. How can I tell? I remember he once talked about handwriting. He said that if you were *used* to a handwriting, the faintest stroke of it was readable. Now I see what he meant. He *was* used to it."

"But the few strokes I can make out are so pale. No one could possibly read that letter."

Charlotte laughed again. "I suppose everything's pale about a ghost," she said.

"Oh, my child, don't say it!"

"Why shouldn't I say it? What difference does it make if her letters are too faint for you and me? Don't you see that she's everywhere in this house? She's even closer to him because she's invisible to everyone else!" Charlotte dropped into a chair and covered her face with her hands. Her sobbing caused her to shake from head to foot. At length, a touch on her shoulder made her look up. She saw her mother-in-law bending over her.

"Tomorrow, tomorrow, you'll see. There will be some explanation tomorrow."

Charlotte cut her mother-in-law short. "An explanation? Who's going to give it, I wonder?"

Mrs. Ashby drew back and stood up straight. "Kenneth himself will," she cried out in a strong voice. Charlotte said nothing, and the old woman went on. "Meanwhile, we must act," she said. "We must tell the police. *Now,* without a moment's delay. We must do everything—everything!"

Charlotte stood up slowly and stiffly. Her joints felt as cramped as an old woman's. "Just as if we thought it could do any good?"

Mrs. Ashby cried, "Yes!" Charlotte went over to the telephone and picked up the receiver.

The Moving Finger

Mrs. Granby was a kind and beautiful woman. Everyone missed her when she died. But how should this beloved woman's memory be kept alive? Two men disagree about her portrait. Which one has the right to decide?

WE USED TO SAY THAT CLAYDON VISITED MRS. GRANCY
TO SEE HER PORTRAIT. HIS ANSWER WAS THAT THE
PORTRAIT *WAS* MRS. GRANCY.

The Moving Finger

I

The news of Mrs. Grancy's death came to me as a shock. Somehow I felt that fate had made a mistake. It wasn't as if Mrs. Grancy had been well-known or important to the world as a whole. It was just that she had filled to perfection her own special place in the world.

Mrs. Grancy's place was her husband's life—and she fitted that space perfectly. If Ralph Grancy's life could be compared to a garden, then his wife was the flower in the middle. Or perhaps she was more like the huge tree at the garden's edge.

Mrs. Grancy gave her husband rest and shade as well as the wind of dreams.

I was one of Grancy's friends. We had all been worried about the man for years. We had seen him fighting one stupid problem after another. Poor health for one, and money trouble for another. But the worst problem he ever had was his first wife. To make herself seem more important, she had kept him as close to her as possible. She nearly drowned the man in affection, as a matter of fact. But just when we thought he was sinking, he would come to the surface again. He might be gasping for air, but then he would again strike out fiercely for the shore.

When at last her death freed him, we wondered how much of Grancy she had taken with her. For a while he seemed numb. But slowly, he began to put out new leaves. Then he met the woman who was to become his second wife. Some of his friends called her his one *real* wife. When he met her, the whole man burst into flower.

The news of Grancy's second marriage had been a shock to us all. After he was burned by his first marriage, we thought he might stay out of the fire. But we agreed that he often made bad mistakes. Now we waited to be introduced to his latest mistake.

Then we met the second Mrs. Grancy. Right away we could see why he had married again. For the first time in years, we could stop worrying about our friend. "He'll do something great now," one of us said. Then another said, "He has already done it—in marrying her."

It was Claydon, the portrait painter, who had said this. Soon after the marriage, Grancy asked Claydon to paint a portrait of his wife. As Claydon painted her, he noticed something very interesting. Mrs. Grancy's face looked like a book of which the last page is never turned. There was always something new to read in her eyes. The portrait showed us all what Claydon read there. When the picture was finished, it was called his masterpiece.

After a year of marriage, Grancy gave up his town house and moved to the country. It seemed sad that we saw him less often, but we all agreed that he deserved his happiness. After all, he had been unhappy for so long.

It wasn't as if they were too far away for us to visit. In fact, our idea of a great day was to visit their place on a Sunday. There we would sit in the Grancys' library and look out at the trees. The portrait of Mrs. Grancy lit up the library wall. We used to say that Claydon visited Mrs. Grancy in order to see her portrait. His answer was that the portrait *was* Mrs. Grancy.

It was interesting that Claydon had such tender feelings for this one portrait. Later we smiled to think of how Claydon would listen when Mrs. Grancy spoke. It was as if he were listening to the picture.

Some human happiness is like a landlocked lake. But the Grancys' happiness was as open as the sea.

There was room to spare on those waters, and we were all happy just to be around them.

II

Three years later, I was in Rome when I heard of her death. The notice said "suddenly." I was glad of that. I was also glad that I was away from Grancy at such a terrible time. I wouldn't have known what to say.

I was still in Rome when he arrived there a few months later. He had taken a job in Constantinople and was on his way there. He told me he took the job "to get away." The job would take a lot of his time, he said, but that was just what he needed. I saw that he was playing a part. He was acting the way he thought a man *should* act in the grip of disaster.

Grief is very powerful. It tends to make us very angry or just give up. But pride makes us want to take a better attitude toward such an enemy. Grancy had chosen the role of the man of action. He was going to make himself too busy to feel pain.

Soon after, my own work called me back home. Grancy stayed in Europe for several years. Then, one summer, I heard that he was back at his place in the country. When I got in touch with him, he invited me to visit the next Sunday. He told me to invite any of our old friends who cared to come.

That very evening, I ran into Claydon at the club. I told him about Grancy's invitation and asked him to come along on Sunday. He said that he already had plans. I was surprised and sorry. Somehow I always thought that he and I were closer to Ralph than the others. If the old Sundays were to be renewed, I thought that Claydon and I should be the first to visit. I said as much to Claydon, but he still said no.

"I don't want to go to Grancy's," he said. I waited a moment, but he didn't explain himself.

"You've seen him since he came back?" I finally asked. Claydon nodded.

I was beginning to get annoyed. I thought that if Claydon knew something about Grancy, he should tell me straight out.

"You've been down there already, I suppose?"

"Yes. I've been down there."

"And are you done with each other? Is the friendship over?"

"Done with each other?" he said. "I wish we were!" Then he stood up and threw down the paper he had been reading. "Look here," he said. "Ralph is the best fellow around. There's nothing under heaven I wouldn't do for him. Nothing, that is, except go to his house again." And with that, he walked out of the room.

I couldn't figure out what would make Claydon act so strangely. But I decided not to ask anyone else to go with me. The next Sunday, I went to Grancy's alone. I was surprised at how my old friend

looked. At the age of 45, he was gray
and bent over. He looked very much like
a tired old man.

Inside the house, nothing looked
changed. I was struck by the sense that
his wife was still there—that I would see
her face at any minute. At lunch time,
Grancy led me to the dining room. There,
the walls, the furniture, and the very
plates seemed like a mirror reflecting her
face. I wondered if Grancy felt the same
way. Did he also sense her nearness?

After lunch, we went for a long walk
through the fields and woods. It was
dusk when we got back to the house.
Grancy led the way to the library. It was
here, at this hour, that his wife had
always welcomed us back.

Since the room faced west, it held a
clear light of its own after the rest of the
house had grown dark. I remembered
Mrs. Grancy. I thought of how young
she had looked in that pale gold light.
Of all the rooms, the library seemed
most completely hers. Here I felt that

her nearness might take a shape we could see. Then, all of a sudden, as Grancy opened the door, that feeling disappeared.

I looked around me. Was the room changed? No. The setting was the same. My feet sank into the same thick rug. The light of the fire bounced off the same rich bindings on the books. Her chair was in its old place by the tea table. From the opposite wall her face gazed at me.

Her face—but *was* it hers? I moved nearer and stood looking up at the portrait.

"You see a change in it?" Grancy said.

"What does it mean?" I asked.

"It means only that five years have passed," he said.

"Over *her*?"

"Why not? Look at me!" He pointed to his gray hair and his wrinkled face. "What do you think kept *her* so young? It was happiness!" He looked up at the portrait tenderly. "I like her better this way. It's what she would have wished."

"Would have wished?"

"Yes. She would have wished for us to grow old together. She would not have wanted to be left behind."

I stood silent, unable to say a word. I looked at the face in the picture. It was not wrinkled like his, but it did seem older somehow. The bright hair had lost its shine. The cheek had lost its youthful glow. The whole woman had aged.

Grancy laid his hand on my arm. "You don't like it?" he said sadly.

"*Like* it? I've lost her!" I burst out.

"And I've found her," he answered quietly.

"In *that*?" I cried.

"Yes, in that. The portrait had become a lie! This is the way she would have looked—*does* look, I mean. Claydon ought to know, don't you think?"

I turned suddenly. "Did Claydon do this for you?"

Grancy nodded.

"Since you got back?"

"Yes. I sent for him after I'd been back a week." He sat down in a chair by the fire. The light fell on his face. He leaned his head back and shaded his eyes with his hand. Then he began to speak.

III

"Surely you could guess what my second marriage meant to me. I needed a pair of eyes that could see with me. I needed a pulse that would keep time with my own. Life is a wonderful thing, of course—a magnificent sight—but I got so tired of looking at it alone.

"Then, I met her. It was like finding the one climate in which I was meant to live. You know what she was like! She lit up the darkness. Oh, you can't imagine how she changed my life! On my way home from work, all I could think of was that she'd be there when I got home.

"When Claydon painted her, he caught the very way she looked at me when I came in. How I loved that picture!

"Three years of happiness, and then she died. It was so sudden that there had been no change in her. Then I went away, as you know, and stayed over there five years. I worked as hard as I knew how. After the first dark months, I came to feel that she was interested in what I was doing. It seemed that she was really *with* me.

"Then I came home. I landed in the morning and came straight down here. The thought of seeing her portrait made my heart beat like a lover's. It was in the afternoon when I opened the library door. The room was full of light. I saw the picture of a young and beautiful woman. But she was smiling at me coldly. I had the feeling that she didn't even know who I was. Then I looked at myself in the mirror. I saw a gray-haired old man whom she had never known!

"For a week the two of us lived together. We seemed like strangers. We were separated by the five years of life that lay between us. Then, slowly, I began to see a look of sadness in the picture's eyes. The look seemed to say, 'Don't you see that *I* am lonely, too?'

"All at once I knew how much she would have hated to be left behind. I remembered something she had said. She had compared life to a heavy book that could not be read unless two people held it together. I thought about how she would have wanted to turn the pages that stood between us!

"Then the idea came to me. It's the *picture* that stands between us. Only the picture is dead—not my wife. To sit in this room is to keep watch beside a dead body. Then the portrait seemed like a beautiful coffin in which she had been buried alive. As this feeling grew, I thought I could hear her beating against the painted walls, crying for help.

"One day, I couldn't stand it any longer. That's when I sent for Claydon. He came down and I told him what I wanted him to do. At first he said no. But the next morning, when I came home from a long walk, I found him sitting here alone. He looked at me and said, 'I've changed my mind. I'll do it.'

"We set up one of the north rooms as a studio, and he worked there for a day. Then he showed me the picture. It stood there as you see it now. I tried to thank him, but he cut me short.

"'There's a train at five, isn't there?' he asked me. 'I have plans for dinner tonight. I have just enough time to make it to the station.' I haven't seen him since.

"I can guess that it was difficult for him to change his masterpiece. But, after all—to him it was only the loss of a picture. To me, it was finding my wife again!"

IV

A few months later, I went back to see Grancy. The first thing I noticed was that the portrait had been moved. It was now in a small study upstairs. He told me he always sat there when he was alone. These days the library was used only for his Sunday visitors. Little by little, all his old friends started coming back to visit. Soon, we were all getting together again on Sunday afternoons. But Claydon never came.

About ten years passed. When I got back one summer from my vacation, I heard that Grancy had been close to death. I hurried down to the country and found him resting. I felt then that he was lost to us, and he read my thoughts.

"Ah," he said, "I'm a sick old man, as you see. I suppose we shall have to slow down now—but we're not ready to go just yet!"

I wondered why he said "we." Without thinking, I looked up at Mrs. Grancy's portrait. Line by line, I saw my fear showing in her face. It was the face of a woman *who knows that her husband is dying*. My heart stood still at the thought of what Claydon had done.

Grancy had followed my look. "Yes, it's changed her," he said quietly. "For months, you know, it was touch and go with me. We had a long fight of it—and it was worse for her than for me." Then he paused and said, "Claydon has been very kind. When I sent for him the other day, he came down at once."

I was silent, and we spoke no more about Grancy's illness. I couldn't help wondering if I would ever see my old friend alive again. But the next time I saw him, he looked much better. Since it was a Sunday, we visited in the library. I did not see the portrait. He continued to improve, and by the spring it looked as if he might recover completely.

One evening, I saw Claydon at the club. "If you're not too busy," I said, "you should go down to Grancy's again."

"Why?" he asked.

"Because he's quite well again," I said. "His wife's fears were wrong."

Claydon stared at me a moment. "Oh, *she* knows," he said with a smile that chilled me.

"You're going to leave the portrait as it is, then?" I asked. He shrugged his shoulders.

About two weeks later, Grancy's housekeeper sent for me. She met me at the station with the news that he had gotten worse. I found him resting in his chair in the little study. He held out his hand with a smile. "You see that she was right after all," he said.

"She?" I asked him, puzzled for the moment.

"My wife." He looked at the picture. "Of course, I knew from the first that she had no real hope that I would get well. I could see that after Claydon had been here. But I wouldn't believe it then."

"Don't believe it now!" I cried out.

He shook his head. "It's too late. I should have known that *she* knew I would die."

"But, Grancy, listen to me," I began, and then I stopped. What could I say to change his mind? After all, it might be easier for him to die, thinking that she *had* known.

V

Grancy's will named me as one of the executors. This made it my duty to tell

Claydon that the portrait of Mrs. Grancy
had been left to him. He said he'd send
for the picture at once. I was staying at
Grancy's house when the portrait was
taken away. After that, I heard nothing
more about the picture for some two
years. I saw Claydon from time to time,
but we had little to say to each other. I
had no real reason to be angry with the
man, but for some reason I resented him.

Then one day, I was talking to a woman
whose portrait Claydon had just painted.
She begged me to go with her to see it. I
was not the only friend she had invited.
The others were all grouped around the
picture when I entered. After admiring
the portrait, I turned away and began to
stroll through Claydon's studio. He was
something of a collector, and his things
were always worth seeing.

The studio was a long room with an
open door at one end. This door opened
into another room that was filled with
books, flowers, fine statues, and vases. I
wandered in and admired a beautiful

blue vase. Then I turned to look at a slender bronze statue. As I did so, I found myself face to face with Mrs. Grancy's portrait.

She smiled at me in all the beauty of youth. The artist had removed every trace of his later work, and the first picture was there. In an instant I recognized that the whole room was a tribute to the portrait. Claydon had put all his best treasures at the feet of the woman he loved. Yes, I saw it clearly now. It was the *woman* he had loved—not the picture. My unexplained anger was now explained.

Suddenly, I felt a hand on my shoulder.

"Ah, how could you?" I cried to him.

"How could I?" he said. "How could I *not*? Doesn't she belong to me now?"

I moved away from him.

"Wait a moment," he said. "The others have gone, and I want to have a word with you. Oh, I know what you've thought of me. I can guess! You think I killed Grancy, I suppose?"

I was quite surprised by his sudden outburst. "I think you tried to do a cruel thing," I said.

"Ah, how little you know!" he said. "Sit down a moment. Here, sit where we can look at her, and I'll tell you something."

Side by side we sat and looked at the portrait.

"In Greek myth, Pygmalion turned his statue into a real woman. I turned my real woman into a picture. You don't know how much of a woman belongs to you after you've painted her! Well, I made the best of it, at any rate. I gave her the best I had in me. And she rewarded me by making me paint as I shall never paint again! There was one side of her, though, that was mine alone. That was her beauty. No one else understood it. Even when Grancy saw the picture, he didn't guess my secret. He was so sure that she was all his! As if a man should think he owned the moon because it was reflected in a pool at his door!

"Think about how I felt when he asked me to change the picture that first time. It was like asking me to commit murder! How could a man who really loved a woman do what he did? How could he ask her to give up her youth and beauty for him?

"At first, I told him I couldn't do it. But later, when he left me alone with the picture, something strange happened. As I sat looking at her, she seemed to say, 'I'm not yours, but his. I want you to make me whatever he wishes me to be.' And so I did it. I could have cut my hand off when the work was done. I'm sure he told you I never went back and looked at it. He thought I was too busy.

"Then last year he sent for me again. It was after his illness. He told me he'd aged 20 years, and he wanted her to grow older, too. He didn't want her to be left behind. At the time, the doctors all thought he was going to get well. I thought so, too, when I first looked at him. But then I looked at the picture.

"I don't ask you to believe me. But I swear it was *her* face that told me he was dying. She wanted him to know it! She had a message for him, and she made me deliver it.

"It seemed cruel at first. But slowly, she made me understand. If she'd been there in person, she seemed to say, wouldn't she have been the first one to see that he was dying? Wouldn't he have read the news in her face? And wouldn't it be horrible if now he should see it instead in strange eyes? Well, that was what she wanted of me. And I did it. I kept them together to the last!" He looked up at the picture again. "But now she belongs to me," he said softly.

Thinking About the Stories

The Pomegranate Seed

1. Look back at the illustration that introduces this story. What character or characters are pictured? What is happening in the scene? What clues does the picture give you about the time and place of the story?

2. Is there a character in this story who makes you think of yourself or someone you know? What did the character say or do to make you think that?

3. Who is the main character in this story? Who are one or two of the minor characters? Describe each of these characters in one or two sentences.

The Moving Finger

1. All stories fit into one or more categories. Is this story serious or funny? Would you call it an adventure, a love story, or a mystery? Is it a character study? Or is it simply a picture the author has painted of a certain time and place? Explain your thinking.

2. Interesting story plots often have unexpected twists and turns. What surprises did you find in this story?

3. Imagine that you have been asked to write a short review of this story. In one or two sentences, tell what the story is about and why someone would enjoy reading it.

Thinking About
the Book

1. Choose your favorite illustration in this book. Use this picture as a springboard to write a new story. Give the characters different names. Begin your story with something they are saying or thinking.

2. Compare the stories in this book. Which was the most interesting? Why? In what ways were they alike? In what ways different?

3. Good writers usually write about what they know best. If you wrote a story, what kind of characters would you create? What would be the setting?

8